# THE POWER of
# COMPLETE
# SURRENDER
## *Living Fully for Christ*

*Offer your bodies as a living sacrifice—*
*holy and pleasing to God.*

# ELLEE RAMAN

Copyright Page

Book title: The Power of Complete Surrender: Living
Fully For Christ
Copyright © 2025 Elishiva Raman
All rights reserved.

Published by:
God's Way Publishing
Greensboro, NC

For permissions or inquiries, contact:
God's Way Publishing
https://sites.google.com/view/gwp2024/home
Godswaypublishing24@gmail.com
+1 (336) 307-0188
Printed in the United States of America

# Table Of Contents:

# Chapter 1: The Call to Surrender – Why God Requires It

**Key Scripture:**
*"Therefore, I urge you, brothers and sisters, in view of God's mercy, to offer your bodies as a living sacrifice, holy and pleasing to God—this is your true and proper worship."* (Romans 12:1 NIV)

## What Does It Truly Mean to Surrender to the Lord Jesus and Why Is It Essential for Our Faith?

To surrender to the Lord Jesus Christ means to willingly lay down our will, our plans, our desires, and even our very lives at His feet. It is the act of yielding complete control to Him—not just in words but in daily actions, choices, and mindset. True surrender requires us to recognize that God knows what is best for us far more than we ever could. It is releasing our need to control outcomes and trusting fully in His perfect will.

Surrender is not a one-time event; it is a continual offering of ourselves as a **living sacrifice**—not dead, but alive and active in our worship through obedience. We choose to walk away from our own self-driven ambitions and embrace His divine purpose for our lives. It is essential because without surrender, we cannot fully receive all that God has for us. Surrender is the doorway to intimacy with Christ, where we stop striving in our own strength and begin to live in the power of His Spirit.

Jesus Himself said in John 15:5, *"I am the vine; you are the branches. If you remain in me and I in you, you will bear much fruit; apart from me you can do nothing."* Without surrender, we remain disconnected, powerless, and vulnerable to the enemy's tactics.

**Key Biblical Examples of Surrender**

Throughout Scripture, we find powerful examples of men and women who surrendered completely to God's will:

**Abraham:**
Abraham's story in Genesis 22 shows the ultimate act of surrender when he was willing to sacrifice his promised son, Isaac. God tested his faith, and because Abraham surrendered, God provided the ram in the bush. Abraham trusted God even when he didn't understand. His surrender paved the way for God's covenant and blessings that still impact us today.

**Jesus:**
The greatest example of surrender is found in Jesus Christ. In the Garden of Gethsemane, as He faced the cross, Jesus prayed in Luke 22:42, *"Father, if you are willing, take this cup from me; yet not my will, but yours be done."* Though fully God, Jesus surrendered His human will to the Father, choosing obedience unto

4

death. Through His surrender, salvation was made available to us all.

**Mary:**

Mary, the mother of Jesus, also demonstrated surrender when the angel Gabriel appeared to her. Though afraid and unsure of what it meant, Mary responded in Luke 1:38, *"I am the Lord's servant...May your word to me be fulfilled."* Her surrender brought forth the Savior of the world.

Each of these examples teaches us that surrender is not easy, but it is always worth it. God uses our surrender to accomplish His greater purpose, far beyond what we can see.

**Surrender vs. Self-Will — Choosing God's Way Over Our Own**

**Key Scripture:**

*"Then Jesus said to his disciples, 'Whoever wants to be my disciple must deny themselves and take up their cross and follow me. For whoever wants to save their life will lose it, but whoever loses their life for me will find it.'"* (Matthew 16:24-25 NIV)

Jesus made it clear that surrender is not optional for us as His followers. To truly be His disciple, we must deny ourselves—that means our self-will, our selfish ambitions, and our fleshly desires. We must pick up our cross daily, which represents dying to our own plans and submitting to God's authority over every aspect of our lives.

Self-will keeps us stuck in cycles of frustration, anxiety, and spiritual dryness. It makes us operate from a place of pride, thinking we know what's best. But when we surrender, we invite the Holy Spirit to lead us, and that's where we find peace, joy, and purpose.

When we hold onto control, we lose the life God intended for us. But when we lose our life for Christ—when we surrender completely—we actually find true life. A life filled with His power, His promises, and His presence.

**Final Thought:** Surrender is the foundation of our faith. Without it, we cannot fully walk in the plans God has for us. True surrender is not a sign of weakness—it is the greatest act of strength because it takes courage to trust God completely.

As we journey through this book, let us reflect on where we are holding back. Are we willing to echo the words of Jesus, *"Not my will, but Yours be done?"*

**Reflection Questions:**

1. In what areas of your life is God calling you to fully surrender?

Take a moment to reflect on the places where you still struggle with control—your relationships, finances, health, or even your dreams. What is God asking you to place on the altar as your living sacrifice?

2. How can you begin to make God's will the priority in your life, and what would that look like on a daily basis?
   Think about the steps you can take each morning to position your heart in surrender—whether it's starting your day in prayer, seeking Him first before making decisions, or inviting the Holy Spirit to lead your thoughts and actions throughout the day.

**Closing Prayer:**

*Lord, Your Word declares in Romans 12:1,* **"I urge you, brothers and sisters, in view of God's mercy, to offer your bodies as a living sacrifice, holy and pleasing to God—this is your true and proper worship."** *I surrender my life to You, offering myself as a living sacrifice. I choose to trust Your will over my own, just as Jesus did, saying,* **"Not my will, but Yours be done."** *(Luke 22:42). Help me to surrender fully, to obey Your Word, to be a doer and not just a hearer, and to walk in Your perfect will. I give You all honor, glory, and praise, in Jesus' name. Amen.*

# Chapter 2: The Struggles That Hinder Surrender

**Key Scripture:**
*"Trust in the Lord with all your heart and lean not on your own understanding; in all your ways submit to Him, and He will make your paths straight."* (Proverbs 3:5-6 NIV)

## Identifying the Most Common Barriers to Surrender

Surrender is not always easy. If we're honest, there are real struggles that make laying down our will difficult. For many of us, the greatest battle is within—fighting the urge to hold on to the things we fear to lose control over. These barriers stand in the way of fully trusting God:

**Fear** — Fear keeps us bound to what is familiar. We fear the unknown, the "what-ifs," and even the cost of surrendering. Fear whispers, *"What if God doesn't come through?"* causing us to pull back when He's calling us forward.

**Pride** — Pride convinces us that we can handle life on our own. It keeps us from asking God for help or admitting we need Him. Pride says, *"I've got this,"* while surrender says, *"Lord, I need You."*

**Control** — Many of us struggle with the desire to control outcomes, people, and situations. Control makes us lean on our own understanding instead of trusting God. It's hard to surrender when we are busy trying to manipulate what only God can handle.

**Doubt** — Doubt creeps in when we forget who God is. It questions His goodness, His timing, and His promises. Doubt makes us hesitate in our surrender, fearing that God won't deliver what He promised.

**Lust** — Lust doesn't just apply to sexual sin—it also represents strong desires for things of the flesh, whether it be wealth, status, or pleasures. Lust pulls us away from surrender because it feeds the flesh instead of the Spirit.

**Past Trauma** — Many of us have deep wounds from our past—betrayals, abuse, rejection, abandonment, or loss—that make it hard to trust anyone, including God. Trauma causes us to build walls to protect ourselves, but those same walls block the flow of surrender.

Each of these barriers is real, but none are bigger than our God. He calls us to trust Him fully and not lean on our limited understanding because He sees what we cannot.

### Biblical Figures Who Struggled but Ultimately Surrendered

Scripture is filled with examples of men who wrestled with surrender but found victory in trusting God:

**Moses:**
When God called Moses from the burning bush to deliver Israel, Moses argued with God, giving excuse after excuse about why he wasn't qualified (Exodus 3-4). Fear, insecurity, and doubt gripped him. Yet God was patient and persistent, proving that Moses didn't have to rely on his own strength. Moses surrendered and became one of the greatest leaders in biblical history.

**Jonah:**
Jonah ran from God's command to go to Nineveh, letting fear, pride, and prejudice guide him. He chose disobedience and ended up in the belly of a great fish. Yet even there, God's patience prevailed. Jonah surrendered, obeyed, and watched an entire city repent and turn to God (Jonah 1-4).

**Peter:**
Peter was bold but often driven by self-will. He swore allegiance to Jesus but denied Him three times out of fear (Luke 22:54-62). Still, Jesus restored him. Peter's surrender came after failure, proving that even when we fall, God is faithful to lift us back up. Peter went on to be a pillar in the early church.

Each of these stories shows us that struggling with surrender is part of the journey—but so is God's relentless grace.

**Encouragement — God Is Patient as We Learn to Surrender**

One of the most beautiful truths we must hold onto is this: God is patient with us. He knows that surrender is a process. He knows our hearts and understands the battles we face. *"The Lord is compassionate and gracious, slow to anger, abounding in love."* (Psalm 103:8 NIV)

The Lord doesn't abandon us when we struggle. Instead, He walks with us, gently teaching us, correcting us, and drawing us closer. *"The Lord is not slow in keeping His promise, as some understand slowness. Instead, He is patient with you, not wanting anyone to perish, but everyone to come to repentance."* (2 Peter 3:9 NIV)

Even when we stumble or pull away, God is there, waiting patiently for us to return. *"Yet the Lord longs to be gracious to you; therefore He will rise up to show you compassion. For the Lord is a God of justice. Blessed are all who wait for Him!"* (Isaiah 30:18 NIV)

Psalm 103:14 reminds us, *"For He knows how we are formed, He remembers that we are dust."* The Lord fully understands our weaknesses, and still, He loves us and extends His grace.

No matter how many times we hesitate, doubt, or wrestle with control, God remains faithful. Surrender is not about perfection; it's about progress. Little by little, day by day, we learn to trust Him fully, resting in His patient love.

**Reflection Questions:**

1. What fears, doubts, or past hurts do you need to surrender to God in order to experience true freedom in Him?
   Take time to identify the specific areas where fear, pride, control, lust, or past trauma have held you back from fully trusting God. Ask the Holy Spirit to reveal them to you. What is keeping you from letting go and placing it all in His hands?

2. How can you lean more on God's understanding and trust Him with the areas where you struggle the most?
   Consider what practical steps you can take to stop relying on your own understanding. How can you begin today to trust God's wisdom, His timing, and His perfect plan for your life?

**Closing Prayer:**

*Father, Your Word tells us in Proverbs 3:5-6, **"Trust in the Lord with all your heart and lean not on your own understanding; in all your ways submit to Him, and He will make your paths straight."** I lay down my fears, selfish desires, doubts, lusts, pride, and past trauma* *before You, trusting that You will guide me and heal me. I thank You for being patient, Lord—for understanding my struggles and never giving up on me. Just as You were patient with Moses, Jonah, Peter, and so many others, I know You are patient with me. Help me to fully surrender, knowing You are faithful and full of grace. May I trust You more each day and walk boldly in the freedom that surrender brings. I praise You for Your mercy, Your love, and Your unending patience. I give You all honor and glory, in Jesus' name. Amen.*

# Chapter 3: The Power Found in Letting Go

**Key Scripture:**
*"Do not be anxious about anything, but in every situation, by prayer and petition, with thanksgiving, present your requests to God. And the peace of God, which transcends all understanding, will guard your hearts and your minds in Christ Jesus."* (Philippians 4:6-7 NIV)

## How Surrender Brings Peace, Freedom, and Spiritual Breakthrough

There is a divine power that comes when we finally let go. Surrendering to the Lord Jesus Christ releases us from the constant pressure of trying to manage life on our own. It frees us from anxiety, fear, and the need to control every outcome. When we let go, we are no longer slaves to circumstances or emotions—we are children of the Most High God, resting in His perfect plan.

The Word reminds us in Philippians 4:6-7 that surrender through prayer and thanksgiving ushers in peace that *"transcends all understanding."* This peace is supernatural—it doesn't make sense to the world. It is the kind of peace that allows us to smile in the middle of storms because we know who is holding us.

**Letting go** is where true freedom lives. We stop wrestling with God and start walking in His promises.

The burdens we once carried become light because Jesus is carrying them for us. He tells us in Matthew 11:28-30, *"Come to me, all you who are weary and burdened, and I will give you rest… For my yoke is easy and my burden is light."* and in 1 Peter 5:7, *"Cast all your cares on Him because He cares for you."* This command alone speaks volumes of His love.

**Knowing God vs. Knowing About Him — Surrender Leads to Deeper Intimacy**

Many of us grow up knowing about God—hearing stories of His power, reading scriptures, and attending church. But it is through surrender that we shift from knowing about Him to truly knowing Him. Surrender takes us deeper. It pulls us into a relationship where we don't just hear His voice—we follow it.

In James 4:8, we are told, *"Come near to God and He will come near to you."* Surrender draws us near because it positions our hearts to receive, to listen, and to be led. The more we surrender, the more intimately we experience God's love, His character, and His presence.

We stop living on surface-level faith and step into a place where God reveals things we could never know in our own strength. Surrender opens doors to spiritual breakthrough—it is the moment where chains fall, strongholds break, and healing begins.

The Holy Spirit is drawn to a surrendered heart. That's where transformation happens. That's where miracles are birthed. That's where we are changed from the inside out.

**Final Thought:** There is power in letting go because we are not losing anything—we are gaining everything in Christ. The peace, the freedom, and the intimacy that come from surrender far outweigh anything this world could offer. As we release our grip on life, God takes over and writes a story greater than we could ever imagine.

**Reflection Questions:**

1. How have you experienced peace or freedom in your life when you have surrendered a particular area to God?

   Take a moment to reflect on a time when you truly let go and trusted God. What did you feel? What did God reveal to you in that season? How did His peace cover you?

2. In what ways can surrender deepen your relationship with God and lead to a more intimate walk with Him?

   Consider what areas you are still holding onto. How might full surrender open the door to hearing God's voice more clearly and experiencing His presence more deeply?

**Closing Prayer:**

*Lord, Your Word says in Philippians 4:6-7,* **"Do not be anxious about anything, but in every situation, by prayer and petition, with thanksgiving, present your requests to God. And the peace of God, which transcends all understanding, will guard your hearts and your minds in Christ Jesus."** *I surrender my anxieties, fears, and the burdens I have carried far too long. I release control and trust You with every detail of my life. I desire not just to know about You, but to truly know You—to walk intimately with You each day. Fill me with Your peace that surpasses all understanding and help me to rest in the freedom that comes from fully letting go. I give You the honor, glory, and praise, in Jesus' name. Amen.*

# Chapter 4: Walking in Daily Surrender – Practical Steps

**Key Scripture:**
*"But seek first His kingdom and His righteousness, and all these things will be given to you as well."* (Matthew 6:33 NIV)

## Making God the Priority—Before Phones, Tasks, or People

Surrender is not a one-time event—it's a daily decision. True surrender requires intentionality. Each morning we wake up, we have a choice: will we seek God first, or will we allow the distractions of this world to consume us?

Jesus commands us in Matthew 6:33 to *"seek first His kingdom and His righteousness"*—not second, not after scrolling social media or jumping into our to-do list, but first. Before we check our phones, answer texts, or engage the world, we must choose to prioritize time with our Father.

When we start our day focused on Him, everything else begins to fall into proper alignment. Our perspective shifts, our burdens lighten, and we are reminded of who we belong to.

**Morning Routine of Surrender—Prayer, Gratitude, Asking for Fresh Anointing**

One of the most powerful habits we can build is a morning routine centered around surrender. Before our feet hit the floor, our hearts should be postured toward God, acknowledging our dependence on Him for the day ahead.

Begin with **prayer**—talk to the Lord honestly, giving Him your day, your thoughts, your plans, and your concerns. Then move into **gratitude**, thanking Him for waking you up, for His mercy, for the blessings you can see and the ones you can't. Gratitude opens the door for His peace and presence.

Finally, **ask for a fresh anointing**. Yesterday's strength won't carry us through today. We need fresh oil, fresh wisdom, and fresh grace daily. Invite the Holy Spirit to lead, guide, and empower you.

Lamentations 3:22-23 reminds us, *"Because of the Lord's great love we are not consumed, for His compassions never fail. They are new every morning; great is Your faithfulness."*

**Seeking the Holy Spirit's Direction and Putting on Spiritual Armor Daily**

Walking in surrender means we don't rely on our own understanding—we seek the Holy Spirit's direction throughout the day. Before making decisions, big or small, pause and ask, *"Holy Spirit, what would You have me do?"*

This is how we stay aligned with God's will. The more we practice it, the more sensitive we become to His voice.

Ephesians 6:11 commands us to ***"Put on the full armor of God, so that you can take your stand against the devil's schemes."*** We cannot walk surrendered if we're spiritually unprotected. Every morning, we must suit up—truth, righteousness, peace, faith, salvation, and the Word of God—ready for the spiritual battles we will face.

**Final Thought:** Daily surrender is a lifestyle, not a task. It's waking up each morning with the mindset, ***"Not my will, Lord, but Yours be done."*** It's understanding that apart from Him, we can do nothing—but with Him, all things are possible.

Every choice we make should reflect the One we serve. We surrender not out of obligation, but out of love and honor for the One who surrendered all for us.

## Reflection Questions:

1.  What changes can you make in your daily routine to prioritize God and surrender your day to Him first?
    Think about your mornings. How can you restructure your start to ensure you are seeking God before everything else—before phones, tasks, or people? What would that look like practically in your life?

2.  How can you actively seek the Holy Spirit's guidance throughout your day and in your decision-making?
    Reflect on your daily moments and decisions. Where do you need to pause more often and invite the Holy Spirit to lead, correct, or confirm your steps? How can you become more intentional about hearing and following His voice?

## Closing Prayer:

*Father, Your Word instructs us in Matthew 6:33, **"But seek first His kingdom and His righteousness, and all these things will be given to you as well."** Help me, Lord, to make You my first priority in every area of my life. Teach me to rise daily with a heart of surrender—praying, giving thanks, and seeking Your fresh anointing. Help me to deny myself, pick up my* *cross, and follow You faithfully, representing You and honoring Your sacrifice with my words, my actions, and my thoughts. Guide me by Your Holy Spirit and lead me in Your will each day. I put on the full armor You have given me, ready to stand in the strength of Your might. I surrender every plan and desire to You, trusting that You know what is best. I give You all glory, honor, and praise, in Jesus' name. Amen.*

# Chapter 5: The Cost of Disobedience & The Rewards of Obedience

**Key Scripture:**
*"But Samuel replied: 'Does the Lord delight in burnt offerings and sacrifices as much as in obeying the Lord? To obey is better than sacrifice, and to heed is better than the fat of rams.'"* (1 Samuel 15:22 NIV)

## The Blessings and Rewards of Obedience

Obedience is the evidence of our surrender to God. It shows our trust, our love, and our reverence for who He is. When we obey, we position ourselves under God's covering and open the door for His blessings to flow.

Jesus said in Luke 11:27-28, *"As Jesus was saying these things, a woman in the crowd called out, 'Blessed is the mother who gave you birth and nursed you.' He replied, 'Blessed rather are those who hear the word of God and obey it.'"*

The Word also reminds us in James 1:22, *"Do not merely listen to the word, and so deceive yourselves. Do what it says."*

Obedience is not about empty religious acts; it is about hearing God's Word and doing what He says. That is where the true blessing lies. God honors our obedience because it shows our faith and dependency on Him.

When we walk in obedience, we see God's promises unfold—we experience His peace, His provision, His protection, and His favor. Obedience leads to open doors, divine connections, answered prayers, and spiritual breakthroughs we could never achieve in our own strength.

## The Consequences of Disobedience

Just as obedience brings blessings, disobedience carries a cost. God is holy and just, and He cannot bless what is contrary to His Word. In Deuteronomy 28, God laid out the clear difference between the blessings of obedience and the curses of disobedience:

*"If you fully obey the Lord your God and carefully follow all His commands I give you today, the Lord your God will set you high above all the nations on earth. All these blessings will come on you and accompany you if you obey the Lord your God."* (Deuteronomy 28:1-2 NIV)

But later, in that same chapter, He warns:
*"However, if you do not obey the Lord your God and do not carefully follow all His commands and decrees I am giving you today, all these curses will come on you and overtake you."* (Deuteronomy 28:15 NIV)

Disobedience opens the door to unnecessary pain, delay, loss, and struggle. It leads us out of God's will and into places where we face the consequences of our own decisions. Sometimes those consequences don't just affect us—they impact our families, our relationships, and our future.

King Saul is a prime example. Instead of obeying God's clear instructions, he chose partial obedience, which was still disobedience. As a result, he lost his kingdom (1 Samuel 15). This shows us that no sacrifice can replace obedience.

**God's Faithfulness to Restore**

Even in our disobedience, God's love remains. He is always ready to restore us when we repent and return to Him. Luke 15:4 reminds us of the heart of our Father:

 ***"Suppose one of you has a hundred sheep and loses one of them. Doesn't he leave the ninety-nine in the open country and go after the lost sheep until he finds it?"***

God pursues us when we wander. He doesn't leave us stuck in the consequences of our disobedience—He comes after us with grace and mercy. The moment we turn back to Him, He forgives, restores, and redeems. That is the beauty of His faithfulness.

No matter how far we've gone or how many times we've disobeyed, God stands ready to receive us, cleanse us, and place us back on the path of blessing.

**Final Thought:** Obedience is better than sacrifice because obedience keeps us connected to God's heart and His will. It positions us to receive all He has for us and protects us from unnecessary suffering.

While disobedience is costly, the reward of obedience is priceless. As we grow in surrender, may we choose obedience daily—trusting that what God has for us is far greater than anything we could ever imagine for ourselves.

**Reflection Questions:**

1. How have you experienced the blessings of obedience in your life, and how can you continue walking in those blessings? Think about times when you obeyed God's voice, even when it was hard. What blessings, peace, or breakthroughs followed? How can you remain consistent in obedience to continue walking in God's favor?

2. Are there areas of disobedience in your life that you need to bring before God for restoration and healing? Take time to examine your heart. Is there anything God has asked of you that you've delayed or refused? How can you surrender those areas now and trust in His faithfulness to restore what was lost?

**Closing Prayer:**

*Lord, Your Word reminds us in 1 Samuel 15:22, **"To obey is better than sacrifice."** I choose to obey Your commands because I know that Your blessings are found in obedience. I trust in Your faithfulness and believe that as I walk in Your ways, You will restore all that has been lost. Help me to be not just a hearer of Your Word, but a doer, walking in faith and complete surrender. May I always choose Your way over my own, knowing that You are a loving Father who only desires the best for me. Thank You for Your mercy, grace, and patience. I honor You, and I give You all praise and glory, in Jesus' name. Amen.*

# Chapter 6: Honoring His Sacrifice Through Our Lives

**Key Scripture:**
*"Therefore, I urge you, brothers and sisters, in view of God's mercy, to offer your bodies as a living sacrifice, holy and pleasing to God—this is your true and proper worship."* (Romans 12:1 NIV)

## Surrender as an Act of Worship—Living Holy Lives

True worship is not just about singing songs or lifting our hands in a service. Worship is a lifestyle—a daily offering of our entire being to God. Romans 12:1 makes it clear that surrender is our "true and proper worship." When we yield our minds, bodies, and will to God, we are worshiping Him in the most powerful way possible.

James 4:7-8 reminds us, *"Submit yourselves, then, to God. Resist the devil, and he will flee from you. Come near to God and He will come near to you."* Surrender invites intimacy with God. It draws us close to Him and separates us from the temptations that seek to pull us away.

Living a holy life doesn't mean being perfect—it means being set apart, choosing obedience over compromise, and seeking to please God in all we do. This is how we honor Jesus—not just with our lips, but with our lives.

**How We Honor Christ's Sacrifice Through Obedience and Love**

Jesus didn't just speak love—He demonstrated it through the cross. The only proper response to such sacrificial love is a surrendered heart that walks in obedience and extends that same love to others.

In John 14:15, Jesus says, *"If you love me, keep my commands."* Obedience is the natural outflow of love. When we love Christ, we honor His sacrifice by living in a way that reflects Him. (If you would like to learn more on this subject, consider checking out my book titled, **"If You Love Me, Keep My Commands"** for sale on Amazon at https://a.co/d/h48YrXB for $5.99/ebook and $7.99/paperback, and https://payhip.com/GodsWayBooks for $5.00/ebook)

Every time we forgive when it's hard, serve without recognition, speak truth in love, or choose righteousness over compromise, we are honoring Him. We carry His name, and we represent His heart to a world that desperately needs Him.

**Denying Ourselves and Carrying Our Cross Daily**

Surrender is not about convenience or comfort. Jesus makes it clear in Luke 9:23, *"Whoever wants to be my disciple must deny themselves and take up their cross daily and follow me."*

Daily surrender means putting God's desires above our own—choosing obedience over comfort, humility over pride, and love over selfishness. It means we make choices that honor and represent Him and His sacrifice, even when it's hard.

We cannot live for ourselves and for Christ at the same time. We must die to our flesh daily so that Christ may live fully through us. That is how we properly honor the price He paid.

To say *"Let Your will be done"* is more than words—it is a declaration of submission. It is choosing to trust God's plan even when it challenges us or costs us something. But in that surrender, we discover deeper joy, purpose, and power than anything we could ever manufacture on our own.

**Final Thought:** Jesus gave everything for us. The least we can do in return is live for Him. When we surrender our lives—our will, desires, and agendas—we are not losing anything. We are giving back what was never ours to begin with and gaining the fullness of His presence in return.

Living in surrender is the highest form of worship. It is how we say, "Thank You" with our lives. May we carry our cross daily, walk in obedience, love boldly, and honor His sacrifice with every breath we take.

## Reflection Questions:

1. How can you live each day as an act of worship, honoring the sacrifice Christ made for you? Take time to reflect on your daily routines, conversations, and decisions. Are they pointing others to Jesus? In what ways can your lifestyle become a living sacrifice that reflects true worship?

2. What does *"carrying your cross"* look like in your life, and how can you embody Christ's love and sacrifice in your actions? Think about the specific areas where God is calling you to deny yourself. How can you say "yes" to His will, even when it challenges your comfort, pride, or preferences?

## Closing Prayer:

*Lord God, Your Word declares in Romans 12:1,* **"Therefore, I urge you, brothers and sisters, in view of God's mercy, to offer your bodies as a living sacrifice, holy and pleasing to God—this is your true and proper worship."** *I surrender my will and desires to You, honoring the sacrifice of Christ. Help me to live daily as an act of love and worship to You, carrying my cross and following You. May my life reflect Your holiness, Your love, and Your truth. I pray that in all I do, I represent*

*You well. Strengthen me to deny myself and walk in obedience, even when it's difficult. I give You the honor, glory, and praise, in Jesus' name. Amen.*

# Chapter 7: Living a Life of Total Surrender – The Eternal Perspective

**Key Scripture:**
*"Whoever wants to be my disciple must deny themselves and take up their cross and follow me. For whoever wants to save their life will lose it, but whoever loses their life for me will find it."* (Matthew 16:24-25 NIV)

### Surrendering to God Prepares Us for Eternity

Surrender isn't just for this life—it is preparation for the life to come. Every time we say "yes" to God and "no" to the flesh, we are aligning our lives with the eternal kingdom that will never fade. Our surrender now is a seed sown for the glory we will one day experience in fullness.

Jesus made it clear—discipleship costs something. It requires denying ourselves, carrying our cross daily, and following Him. But that cost is nothing compared to the reward: eternal life in His presence, eternal joy, and a crown of righteousness.

This life is temporary. Our homes, careers, titles, and achievements will pass away, but what we do for Christ will last forever. Jesus reminds us in Matthew 6:19-20, *"Do not store up for yourselves treasures on earth,*

*where moths and vermin destroy, and where thieves*
*break in and steal. But store up for yourselves treasures*
*in heaven, where moths and vermin do not destroy, and*
*where thieves do not break in and steal."*

Total surrender shifts our mindset from earthly gain to
heavenly purpose. It positions us to live with eternity in
mind, not just momentary comfort.

## The Long-Term Blessings of Surrender—Walking in God's Power, Favor, and Purpose

When we surrender our lives to God, we begin to walk in
alignment with His perfect will. And with that surrender
comes His power—strength to endure, authority to
overcome, and grace to walk boldly in our calling.

Surrender invites the favor of God into our lives. We may
not always understand where He's leading us, but we can
be confident that His path is filled with divine
appointments, provision, and purpose.

We were never meant to live life in our own strength.
That's why Jesus sent the Holy Spirit—to lead, guide,
comfort, and empower us. Surrendering daily to the
Spirit positions us to fulfill our kingdom assignment with
supernatural effectiveness.

Proverbs 19:21 says, *"Many are the plans in a person's*
*heart, but it is the Lord's purpose that prevails."* When

we surrender our plans to God, we make room for His purpose to prevail.

**Final Call to Action—Fully Commit to Surrendering Your Life to God**

This journey of surrender is not easy, but it is essential. It requires daily decisions, intentional living, and unwavering trust in God's goodness and sovereignty.

Let this be your moment to say, *"Lord, I surrender all."* Your future, your relationships, your gifts, your fears—place them all in His hands. Commit fully to a life that honors Jesus not just with words, but with obedience, love, and faith.

When we live surrendered, we live free. When we live surrendered, we live with purpose. And when we live surrendered, we live prepared for eternity.

Choose today to live fully for Christ. Let your life be the testimony that says, ***"Not my will, but Yours be done."***

**Reflection Questions:**

1. How does the eternal perspective shape the way you view surrender in your everyday life? Consider how the promise of eternity changes your priorities. Are you investing more in temporary things or eternal ones? What adjustments can you

make to live with heaven in view?

2. What are some steps you can take today to live more fully surrendered to God, with eternity in mind?
Think practically—what can you surrender right now that's been standing between you and full obedience? How can you start each day with eternity as your focus, choosing to seek God's will above your own?

**Closing Prayer:**

*Lord, Your Word says in Matthew 16:24-25,* **"Whoever wants to be my disciple must deny themselves and take up their cross and follow me."** *I choose to surrender fully, knowing that it is through surrender that I gain life in You. Holy Spirit, may You fill me with Your fruit that I may live as Jesus lived. Help me to live each day with eternity in mind—not chasing after fading treasures, but storing up what pleases You. Strengthen me to walk in Your purpose, to obey Your voice, and to reflect Your heart in everything I do. May my life be fully Yours. I give You all the glory, honor, and praise, in Jesus' name. Amen.*

# Closing Chapter: The Final Surrender – Living Fully for Christ

Throughout this journey, we have been called to one central truth: complete surrender to the Lord Jesus Christ is not just a suggestion—it is the foundation of a life that pleases God. From the moment we first say "yes" to Him, surrender becomes the heartbeat of our faith.

We began by exploring **why God requires surrender**—because He is holy, sovereign, and worthy of our entire lives. We looked at biblical examples of men and women who said yes to God's will above their own and were forever transformed.

We learned that **the greatest battles against surrender happen within us**—fear, pride, lust, doubt, and past trauma try to keep us bound. But even in those struggles, God is patient and faithful to guide us toward freedom.

We discovered that **there is supernatural power in letting go**—peace that surpasses understanding, intimacy with the Lord, and divine rest that can only be found in His presence. Surrender opens the door to deeper relationship.

We explored the **daily disciplines of surrender**—starting our mornings with prayer, gratitude, and fresh anointing; seeking the Holy Spirit's direction;

and putting on the full armor of God. Each day offers a new opportunity to say, *"Not my will, Lord, but Yours be done."*

We faced the reality that **disobedience carries a cost**, but obedience brings blessing. Yet even when we've fallen short, God's grace is more than enough to restore, redeem, and set us back on the right path.

And we were reminded that **living a surrendered life is how we honor Christ's sacrifice**—through holiness, obedience, love, and carrying our cross daily. When we deny ourselves and represent Jesus well, we glorify the One who gave everything for us.

Finally, we were challenged to **live with eternity in mind**—to surrender not just for today but forever. What we do now echoes into eternity. And every act of obedience builds treasure in heaven that will never fade.

### The Call to Action: Will You Surrender All?

Now the choice is yours.
 Will you live for yourself—or for Christ?
 Will you hold onto control—or lay it all down at His feet?
 Will you chase temporary rewards—or invest in eternal glory?

The Lord is calling each of us to a deeper level of surrender. Not just on Sundays. Not just in crisis. But every single day.

This is not a moment—it is a lifestyle.
 This is not religion—it is relationship.
 This is not weakness—it is victory.

Jesus gave everything for you. He held nothing back. He took the nails, the shame, the cross, and the weight of all our sin—and He did it in love.

Now He stands with open arms, waiting for your full surrender.

So today, right now, wherever you are—make the decision to live fully for Christ. Not halfway. Not when it's convenient. But completely.

Lay down your fear, your pride, your pain, your dreams, your plans—and pick up your cross.

Walk in the power of surrender.
 Walk in the purpose of His will.
 Walk in the love of your Savior.

And never look back!!!

## Final Reflection Questions:

1. What areas of your life have you been holding back from fully surrendering to God, and what steps can you take today to release them into His hands?

   Be honest with yourself and with the Lord. What have you feared letting go of? What is keeping you from trusting Him completely? What does full surrender look like in your life starting now?

2. How can you live each day with eternity in mind, walking in obedience, carrying your cross, and honoring Christ's sacrifice?

   Think about how your daily choices reflect the life of someone living for eternal purpose. What routines, decisions, or mindsets need to shift to align with the life of total surrender?

## Final Closing Prayer:

*Lord Jesus, I thank You for the gift of surrender. Your Word declares in Matthew 16:24-25,* ***"Whoever wants to be my disciple must deny themselves and take up their cross and follow me. For whoever wants to save their life will lose it, but whoever loses their life for me will find it."*** *I choose today to lose my life for Your sake, that I may find true life in You. I surrender my will, my ways,* *my worries, and my desires. I lay them all down at Your feet.*

*Forgive me for the times I've walked in my own understanding, chasing things that fade. Help me to live each day with eternity in mind—anchored in Your love, filled with Your Spirit, and led by Your truth. May my life be a living sacrifice, holy and pleasing to You, a true act of worship.*

*I say yes to Your call. Yes to Your will. Yes to Your way. May my heart stay bowed, my hands stay open, and my life reflect the power of complete surrender.*

*I give You all the honor, glory, and praise, in Jesus' name. Amen.*

# Author's Note

I dedicate this book to every soul who longs to live in the fullness that Christ freely offers. To those who are tired of shallow religion and ready to dive into deep relationship. To every soul who is hungry for more—more of God's presence, more of His power, more of His purpose. To the surrendered ones and to the ones still learning how to let go—this is for you.

This is for the one who has wrestled with control, battled fear, or felt stuck in cycles of disobedience. For the one who has tasted grace but longs for deeper intimacy with the Father. For the one who is ready to lay it all down—not out of obligation, but out of love. This book is for every heart that desires to know Jesus more, to trust Him fully, and to walk in the blessings of a life yielded to His perfect will.

*"Whoever wants to be my disciple must deny themselves and take up their cross daily and follow me."* (Luke 9:23 NIV)

My prayer is that these pages have stirred something eternal in you—a desire to walk in true surrender and experience the blessings, peace, and power that come when we give God our everything.

Complete surrender is not the end—it's the beginning of the most beautiful, purposeful, and fulfilling journey you will ever take. It is the exchange of our limited understanding for His limitless grace. And it is the only way to experience true peace, lasting joy, and eternal impact.

This is the life Jesus calls us to—not one of bondage, but of freedom through surrender.

May this book inspire you to pursue Him with your whole heart and never look back.

With all my love and surrendered heart,
**Ellee Raman**
*Founder, God's Way Publishing*

Made in the USA
Middletown, DE
01 April 2025

73601482R00026